Sarah

Reading

Love Suzie
xo

July
2021

REFRESH

Illustrations by Nel Whatmore

This is a FLAME TREE Book

FLAME TREE PUBLISHING
6 Melbray Mews, Fulham,
London SW6 3NS, United Kingdom
www.flametreepublishing.com

First published 2019

19 21 23 22 20
1 3 5 7 9 10 8 6 4 2

ISBN: 978-1-78755-686-7

Edited by Nel Whatmore
Poems and quotes by Nel Whatmore are © Nel Whatmore 2019
All images © Nel Whatmore 2019.
Licensed by Nel Whatmore.
www.nelwhatmore.com

The cover image is *Up Up and Away* by Nel Whatmore.

A copy of the CIP data for this book is available from the British Library.

Printed and bound in China

REFRESH

Illustrations by Nel Whatmore

THOUGHTS TO INSPIRE & MOTIVATE

FLAME TREE
PUBLISHING

REFRESH

Illustrations by Nel Whatmore

Refresh: Thoughts, Quotes and Poetry

Artist at Work: Nel Whatmore

An insight into the working methods, influences

and studio of a remarkable artist.

It's humbling to start fresh. It takes a lot of courage. But it can be reinvigorating. You just have to put your ego on a shelf and tell it to be quiet.

Jennifer Ritchie Payette

You get in life what you

have the courage to ask for.

Oprah Winfrey

Every time I see you
it feels like a new
day, with endless
possibilities and a
million games to play.

Nel Whatmore

Life is not measured
in breaths, but in how
many moments take
our breath away.

Vicki Corona

If you love something,
it will work. That's the
only real rule.

Bunny Williams

When the sky is
THAT blue
The one it's hard
to replicate
And each cloud is
freshly made
Like whipped cream
upon a cake

The grass tickles toes
Thirsty for the rain
Your shoes slipped off
Remember the child in
you again

Nel Whatmore

To dream is not

the pastime of fools,

But the act of

a generous mind,

Too ample to fill

its allotted slot.

It creates a place

without limits,

Where freely it can shine

Nel Whatmore

Pause for thought

And watch the clouds

scudding by

Life is reflected in the

deep blue dye

Plants dip their leaves

Into the mysterious well

And bend their reflection

In search of stories to tell

Nel Whatmore

It's never too late – never
too late to start over, never
too late to be happy.

Jane Fonda

Let go of what you know,
trust that it will be your
silent guide. Reach for
the stars and see the world
as if you were a child.

Nel Whatmore

You can learn new things at any time in your life if you're willing to be a beginner. If you actually learn to like being a beginner, the whole world opens up to you.

Barbara Sher

The challenge is to restore
the home of the tadpoles
and give back to our
children a world of
beauty and wonder.

Wangari Maathai

If people are doubting how far you can go, go so far that you can't hear them.

Michele Ruiz

It's not about the big
things, its about finding
beauty in the simple things.

Nel Whatmore

Work less than you think
you should... And nap: it
helps to refresh the brain.
Amy Waldman

The secret to change is to focus all of your energy, not on fighting the old, but on building the new.

Dan Millman (Way of the Peaceful Warrior)

It's not about finding
the perfect moment to
change, but finding the
time to see that every
moment is a change.

Nel Whatmore

The heaviness of being successful was replaced by the lightness of being a beginner again, less sure about everything. It freed me to enter one of the most creative periods of my life.

Steve Jobs

Pausing for thought allows your body to rest and your mind to decide where it wants to go next.

Nel Whatmore

Learn from yesterday,

live for today, hope

for tomorrow.

Anon

If you have no
direction, start by
planting something
that will grow.
Nel Whatmore

Summer is in full flush

Fresh and verdant green

Turning its myriad faces

All craning to be seen

Nel Whatmore

Reasons to be cheerful

Lovely things to do

A thousand little treats

my friends

All waiting just for you

Nel Whatmore

Dull days can be the prelude to your most colourful ones.

Nel Whatmore

Start by doing what's necessary, then do what's possible, and suddenly you're doing the impossible.

Anon

A woman who cuts her hair
is about to change her life.

Coco Chanel

Sunshine on a stalk,

that's a daffodil to me

Painting the earth yellow

as far as you can see

They herald a new spring,

they bow and welcome in

They are greeted with relief,

like hot tea or ice-cold gin!

Nel Whatmore

I realize there's something incredibly honest about trees in winter, how they're experts at letting things go.

Jeffrey McDaniel

Joy!

Great goblets of joy!
They fill the heart up
Their lustrous petals
Bend and sip from
their cup

Bursting like fireworks
Explosions of red
Colour cascading
In rich flower beds

Blousy and rich
Or pale and refined
There is nothing so brilliant
They are one of a kind

Nel Whatmore

I walk with you behind

my eyes,

On warm sunny days

below a cerulean sky

Nel Whatmore

Looking at the world in a
different light, takes us down
a different path that was
obscured and out of sight.

Nel Whatmore

You are never too old to set another goal or to dream a new dream.

Les Brown

Change can be scary, but you know what's scarier? Allowing fear to stop you from growing, evolving, and progressing.

Mandy Hale

We should concern ourselves not so much with the pursuit of happiness, but more with the happiness of pursuit.

From Hector and the Search for Happiness

I am a secret tree hugger

I've loved them from a child

Along with shiny pebbles

Collected at low tide

From a perfectly placed seed

To a trunk I now embrace

Their warmth fills me

for a moment

Their calm, their age,

their grace

Nel Whatmore

Everyone has a voice,

from those who shout

To those who are as

quiet as a mouse

What matters to you

And shapes your world

Is always worth

standing up for

Be brave

Be bold

Be beautiful

Walk Tall

Nel Whatmore

I walk in a garden

And my soul lies back

My lungs fill like sails

My shoulders relax

My heart strings are pulled

By the scent of the breeze

My thoughts gently gathered

My worries kindly eased

Nel Whatmore

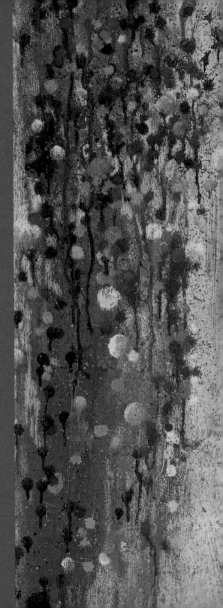

Let it go

Like a kite

That pulled so tight

And blew away

The spool

The reel

The rot

The curled-up knot

That makes you stop

Fling it high

And scream it out

And shout and run about

Let it play and have

its way

Let it go... is what I say

Nel Whatmore

Sometimes life is complicated, but every piece is still part of a beautiful whole... you just need to stand back.

Nel Whatmore

Salmon sliver clouds bid

the day good night.

I thank all my lucky stars

you are my friend tonight.

Nel Whatmore

A wildflower meadow

conjures memories for me

Of all that I was, but

now all that I see

Of the patience that grows

and the time I now give

To relish the small things

in the world that we live

Nel Whatmore

A risk is not scary, it's just a

choice to change, to learn

and embrace what our fears

don't want us to discover.

Nel Whatmore

Saying the same thing
every day, like 'I love
you', is not to render
it meaningless, but
every day to convey
the inexpressible
through repetition.

Nel Whatmore

Every raindrop saves a
life, creates a dream,
makes an ocean, a sea
of hope.
Nel Whatmore

Forget about the fast lane.

If you really want to fly,

harness your power to

your passion.

Oprah Winfrey

Artist at Work: Nel Whatmore

All my most vivid early memories are of creating things: sticking and glueing, making paper hats, and art lessons at school that I wanted to go on all day. My parents encouraged me by allowing me to paint murals on my bedroom wall and regularly change everything – from printing my duvet covers to batiking wall hangings. My Dad bought me my first easel, which seemed like a big deal at the time.

Life in the Studio

My studio is at the top of our house away from my husband who needs complete quiet to write. I play the radio or music loudly and light streams in from my north-facing windows. I have taken advantage of my low ceiling and written poems, phrases and lyrics on it. Friends and family now leave me thoughts that way too!

I don't rise at six and paint until noon, as I am not one for routine – or early mornings! One of the great joys of being an artist is that every day is different and variety is in itself inspiring. I do usually try to paint for quite a few hours at a time, as I find it is only through painting for longer periods that I really improve.

I work in pastels mostly but also mixed media. I often do an underpainting using pastel primers and acrylics and then work into that when it is dry. I love the fluidity of paint but the colours and immediacy of pastels. There is something about holding pure pigment in stick form,

rather than being at the end of a brush, that suits me best. I keep things fresh by changing my subject matter in cycles in order to return to subjects with renewed enthusiasm. I like setting myself specific challenges – for instance, this year my focus is to study water for a series called 'The Wonders of Water'. I also have times when I just play around and try to discover new ways of working. The painting *Up Up and Away* (a detail of which is on the front of this book) was produced on just such a day.

Inspiration, Expression and Reception

Having had personal and family health troubles, our perspective on life is simply that it is very very precious. We have learnt not to hesitate to do things and enjoy the smallest things. Life and all its ups and downs infuse my work. As someone once said to me, 'you are what you paint'. But I have learnt to use my painting as a very cathartic thing and I aim not only to convey the beauty of the natural world, to make people stop, look and think, but also to convey a little of the inexpressible. For me the arts are there to celebrate the good and be salve to the soul. The effect that colour has on our emotions and its importance in different cultures fascinates me. I find certain colours uplifting, and hope that through my paintings they do the same for the viewer. Music plays a large part in my work, as I choose different styles of music to evoke different emotions.

My paintings and poems are an expression of me at a moment in time. They do seek to convey a little of what it means to be human and all that we hold dear as well

as strive for. How they are received I have no control over, I can only say that I am encouraged that I have been told many times that my work makes people feel good... and if that is the result of all the hours spent painting and looking and reworking and looking again, then that is good enough for me.

Advice for Budding Artists

Determination, tenacity and being good at multitasking are probably the most useful personality traits. Be true to your heart and paint what makes you happy, set yourself goals, be professional, cultivate good relationships. I started off selling my work on a market 33 years ago and I still have many of the customers I met then, and best of all, they are lifelong friends.

THOUGHTS TO INSPIRE & MOTIVATE